Lean In

Poems of the Heart by

Beth Bricker Davis

To Donna —
with love + friendship —
Beth

Dedication

For my dear friend Jerome, one of my very staunchest supporters. Jerome has thoughtfully read my poems though the years and offered constant encouragement, insight, support, and friendship. For all of these things I am eternally grateful.

Also for my amazing "Coffee Friends," who are a force of nature and are some of the most worthwhile people in the world. They have helped me to "Lean In" to love, compassion, and hope as we share our incredible life journeys. Thank you Annette, Debbie, Diane, Jan, Joyce, Jude, Linda, and Margie.

Cover Photo by Beth Bricker Davis. Photo taken at the beautiful Nature and Raptor Center of Pueblo.

About the Author photo by Ross Barnhart

ISBN-13:
978-1534738416

ISBN-10:
153473841X

Books also by Beth Bricker Davis:

Aspen Leaves in October,
Poems of Life, Love, and Loss.

Acknowledgments

With love and gratitude to –

My good friend Rev. Jude LaFollette, BCC, who kindly read most of the poems in *Lean In* and served as a thoughtful "pre-editor" for a second time, as well as a loyal friend.

Raven Agape, who, also for a second time, offered outstanding formatting and publishing expertise, and to Amy Agape, who, once again, skillfully served as the final editor for one of my books.

Friends and family members have offered constant emotional support and occasional literary input. To all of you I am deeply grateful! To try and list them all would be to exclude someone. If you have crossed my path in a caring manner or offered encouragement on my writing journey, I am grateful! Thank you.

Preface

All of the poems in *Lean In* were written as I "leaned into" my heart, as I paid attention to the feelings that my life experience evoked, including my experience of the world at large. The poems are based in love, awareness of my own mortality, and compassion for those who suffer.

A few of the poems in *Lean In* were written for friends, and I am grateful for their permission to use those poems in this book. When a poem was written for a friend, that is noted following the poem.

I am grateful to my dear friend Joyce Spears who suggested the book's title, *Lean In*, which is part of a phrase from the poem, *What If This is Not the Last?* from the chapter, *Lean Into Hope.*

It is always my hope that my poems will offer comfort, healing, validation, or insight. With a firm belief that we are all undeniably connected, as per the lines from the poem, *Thoughts I Cannot Share*; "... there is a part of that guy in me and a part of me in him..." May we honor the qualities we all share.

Table of Contents

Lean Into Love

Even Though You Left

Dear Husband,
even though you left,
walks along the Arkansas River at dusk
are still
beautiful.

Water still
rushes quietly
over smooth boulders and
V–formed flocks of geese still
fly overhead, honking and splashing down
into the cold water,
searching for food,
tending to
one another,
gently floating together
downstream
with the swift current.

Dear Mother,
even though you left,
the love you gave me still
lives in my heart.

Christmas decorations,
your favorite, are still
bright and shiny.
Red gleaming tree bulbs and
animated figurines
singing happy Christmas carols still
make me smile, still
bring me joy.

Dear Father,
even though you left,
sweet strawberries still
grow in the beautiful garden
you tended.

Long car rides
in the quiet countryside still
bring me peace,
watching grazing cattle
and beautiful horses
stomping their hoves,
swatting flies impatiently
with their bushy tails.

Lengthy visits
to the candy store,
lingering over the chocolate counter still
brings me happiness, still
makes me glad
for the sweet tooth we shared.

Dear Friend,
even though you left,
social gatherings are still
dear, your silly giggle still
echoes in my mind, happily
taking me to your farm where
October leaves crunch
under the wagon wheels
of a hayride.

Farmers still
plant and till and
fields of hearty grain still
flourish under a hazy blue sky,

reaching their tender leaves
upwards and around
each other where together,

everyone I love
quietly waits,

my husband,
my mother,
my father,
my friend.

Even though you left,
your beauty still
lives
in my world.

One Long, Full, Beautiful Day

The chirping crickets
outside my bedroom window
this warm spring night
take me to my happy childhood and
memories of
my long, lanky Uncle Dan, who drank
an eight-ounce glass of whole milk
every night before bed.

I can still see him
standing tall
on the cold kitchen tile
of their Muncie, Indiana,
country home
in his suede moccasins and
long pajamas and terry cloth blue robe while

our sweet Aunt Mary readied
their twin beds
in the long bedroom
at the back of their
Indiana limestone house.

Mom and I trudged
up the steep wooden stairs
to the moonlit dormer bedroom
without awareness
of the stillness of the night or of
the deep ebony
of the country sky
sprinkled with bright white stars.
twinkling silently overhead
while we slept.

My Uncle Dan,
the glass of milk,
the cold tile,
my sweet Aunt Mary,
the twin beds,
my dear mom,
those steep stairs,
and that impossibly
black sky and white twinkling stars are
etched
forever in my heart and mind,

sometimes re-appearing quietly
in my dreams
or in my words
like the wispy smoke
of a burned-out campfire
slowly drifting with the breeze
towards the still lake
at the end of
one long, full, beautiful day.

If This Were My Last Day

If this were my last day
I would surround myself with a few
sweet dogs, quiet dogs,
Golden Retrievers or Labs,
or perhaps Shi Tzu's or Dauschunds,
the kind of dogs who would nestle
themselves comfortably
around me, nudging themselves gently
under my forearms, brushing themselves
tenderly
against my cheeks, pressing against
my tired, tired legs, soothing me with their
warm,
quiet bodies and the softest, softest coat.

If this were my last day,
dear, dear friends and family,
just a few, or maybe
many, would come,
quietly into and out of
my sleepy room,
taking my soft hand,
brushing the brown hair from my pale
forehead,
sometimes smiling, sometimes
weeping softly,
sometimes laughing,
telling sweet stories of beautiful string music
and
amazing card games long into the night and
blissful times fishing on the banks of
beautiful, peaceful lakes
in southern Indiana.

If this were my last day,
there would be meaning-
ful poetry readings and
beautiful artwork around me, and
lovely Baroque music filling the air,
Handel, Mozart, Corelli, Vivaldi, Bach,
drifting softly over my bed,
into the hallways,
circling my friends and family, drifting
out the door, and into
the quiet, sunlit yard.

And for my beloved visitors,
large, hand-crafted, colorful ceramic bowls of
fine chocolates and cashews,
chilled mandarin oranges and
chunks of fresh pineapple
served with delicious sparkling sweet
Champagne,
or for the have-nots,
sweet sparkling juice.

If this were my last day,
I would fade quietly away
with slowly deepening,
comfortable, peaceful breaths and
the dogs would still themselves,
listening
for my last, long, quiet sigh and
nestle snugly against my chest,
pressing me closer to
the other side,
gently wagging their tails in relief as
my spirit left,

sweetly licking my face and hands and the hands
of my visitors,
assuring them of
my spirit's new-found peace and of
my next, joy-filled journey.

The Christmas Mom Broke Her Clavicle

Standing alone in my quiet kitchen,
this Christmas Eve 2015,
listening to the Denver classical radio station
in my southern Colorado home, I
close my eyes to the angelic
Christmas carols coming from the speakers
and see

Mike and me making our way through
the long snow-covered driveway
of my Indiana childhood home
in our green Jeep Cherokee,
my pink-robed elderly mother asleep
in her family room lounge chair,
anxiously awaiting our Christmas Day arrival,
TV remote fallen to her side, as
we trudged from the car through the snow
to the house, rapping briskly on the cold
window pane
for Mom to unlock the small metal garage
door.

Mom awakened with a start and before
she could realize that her robe was caught
in the fold of her velour recliner,
or before she could remember that
she was no longer 30,
she leapt up, falling quickly to the floor.

We stood helplessly outside
the window, covered in heavily falling snow
as

Mom disappeared from sight
for a minute and I feared the worst.
Mike insisted he was breaking down
the door before I saw Mom rise slowly
from the floor, somehow, making her way
down the inside garage steps, across the cold
concrete floor
to unlock the little door for us.

We brushed the snow from
our coats and hats and followed Mom
carefully
back into the warm house
where she gingerly returned
to her soft recliner

Are you okay, we asked, do you want
to go to the emergency room?

Mom was her sweet, quiet, stoic self but said
her shoulder hurt. She thought
she would be okay if she just
went to bed. I know
my mom and I know
she was more troubled by the fact that
she had ruined our perfect reunion
than the fact that she had probably
injured herself.

I pulled the sleeve of her robe away
to look at her frail little body,
but what did I know? The coloring was the
same,
and I couldn't tell if anything had moved.

It was already late, 9:30 or so,

and already past Mom's
8:00 bed time. It was so hard
for her to wait up for us but
the weather had made for a late start
from Vincennes, where we had already
celebrated
Christmas Eve with Mike's family.

It was snowing like crazy and I knew
if we went to the emergency room,
we'd be there all night. Mom was so little
and tired and old, we all decided
to go to bed, praying it was
a good decision.

The next day, it was still snowing like crazy,
but Mom was still hurting,
so we headed to Dr. Kumar's office
and on to the ER, where he sent us,
and where they diagnosed her fractured
clavicle.

They put a blue fabric sling
over her dominant left arm and hours later,
off we went, back to her warm family room
and colorful ceramic Christmas tree.

We had to leave Mom's house after only
a few days and made her show us
that she could independently
don and doff her shoulder sling.
I don't know how she did it,
how she kept on living
alone in that old house
for as long as she did, but no

broken clavicle was going to change
her standard of living or make her
ask for help when she would do everything
she could to
do it herself.

Mom died over five years ago now.
I still think back to that day, and others,
and apologize for not
taking her to the ER that night or for not
staying longer then or not staying longer
after she had her bleeding ulcer or
for staying too long in her room
at Sterling House when she was very old and
very frail and probably would have rested
better
had I not stayed so long.

This thing about staying or going,
whether it's to the ER or
someone's house or
staying in someone's life
catches me off guard sometimes,
so I listen
to the radio or watch passing clouds or
look to the full moon with the hope that
someday,
it will all make sense.

He Was Hooked

From the moment her pudgy little hand
wrapped itself around his index finger,
he was hooked. He knew it.
His heart raced a little and
before he even tried to stop them,
huge, wet tears were running down
his flushed cheeks,

dripping onto her blanket,
dripping onto his wife's hospital bed,
dripping onto his Nike tennis shoes,
the same shoes he had been wearing
for two and a half days while
his wife labored to bring
their first child,
their first beautiful little girl,
into the universe.

The tears were not
the same tears he cried when
his high school basketball team
lost the state tourney,
or the kind of tears when
he broke his arm
wrestling with his big brother
when he was ten, but instead

these tears came
from a part of his heart
he never knew
existed. A part that had suddenly
opened, changed in a way that
he could not describe,

an eagle spreading its glorious wings,
the singing of the "Hallelujah Chorus,"
a bright galaxy expanding
into the infinity of space.

He saw his little girl's life
flash before his eyes,
the soft pink blankets and teddy bears,
the midnight feedings and multiple,
multiple diaper changes,
the high temperatures and nights of worry,
pacing in the dark, rocking her until
she quieted, the silent relief when
her eyes brightened and she
smiled again,

the tutus and trucks, the skinned knee after
her first fall off of her tricycle,
the first day of school and the look of terror
in her eyes, her small hands clinging
to his pant leg,
her first school friend and the two of them
skipping sweetly down the sidewalk, arm-in-
arm,
singing a made-up song,

the first nervous parent-teacher conference,
and the pride they all shared for her first
gold star on her homework paper,

her first swim competition and first
blue ribbon, and her slamming-door tears
when
she won no ribbon at all,

their first father–daughter dance, and the way
they practiced a waltz, the stars in her eyes
for him alone until
her first boyfriend, and then, her first broken
heart,

her high school graduation and the way
she smiled smartly, walking with ease
across the stage, waving at her tearful,
smiling parents before
off to college she drove, and now this,

this new man who took her hand and her
heart
and there her dad stood,
at the beginning of a long,
satin cloth–lined aisle with his little girl
on his arm and with the unspeakable thought
that he could not possibly
give her away to some man who had never
experienced the exquisite grip of her pudgy
little hand
on his index finger.

The Year Mr. Tyndall Died Before My Mom

It was 2009.
Mom had celebrated
her 99th birthday a few months before,
survived and healed from yet another
fracture and
we were sitting in the sunlit bedroom
of her assisted living facility,
on a warm September afternoon,
me, uncomfortably on Mom's bed,
Mom, uncomfortably in her wheelchair.

Mom hated being
in that wheelchair.
There were not enough pillows in the world
to protect the frail skin and fragile bones of
her tiny frame and besides,
she would rather be vigorously walking.

We were sitting close,
facing each other, not just because
we loved each other deeply, but so
Mom could read my lips, a skill she had
developed rather keenly
in the last year or so.

The topic was birthdays.
If they made it,
Mom, and her good friend Katie,
whom Mom had known her whole life,
and who was three weeks younger,
would both make the century mark the next
summer.

We were marveling
at their long devoted friendship and
their long lives and I asked Mom
Do you think you will live to be 100?
knowing full well it was only about
ten months away but also knowing that
Mom had already lived way past
her statistically allotted time.

Well that's a depressing thought! Mom said,
and so
we changed the topic to the weather or the
dinner menu or
something of little consequence.

The calendar pages kept turning and
before we knew it, it was 2010.
Mom was tired. Everything was harder and
everything hurt. Being helped from her
wheelchair was
excruciating and even though Mom tried
to be patient and thank
everyone, even though she didn't say it until
months later, I think
she was ready to go.
I think she would have felt relieved to have
laid down in her quiet single bed and not
awakened
the next morning.

In February,
my dear friend's father,
77 year–old Mr. Tyndall, who was
larger than life, died
in his sleep

next to his devoted wife in their
downtown apartment with his
"to-do" list on the nightstand
by his bed.
Still planning for the next day and for
the days after.
We were all shocked because Mr. Tyndall was
not
my mom.
He was not 99. He did not appear to be
tired of living or anxious for
a reprieve from a tired, pained body.
But, his heart was challenged, and
it was not the first time he had
flirted with death, having had heart surgery
years before.
77 years of exuberant living had taken its toll
and
he was a man, after all,
he wasn't supposed to live
into his 90's.

Mom began failing as spring rolled around,
eating less, sleeping more, weakly pounding
her bedroom walls
with her tiny fist,
in frustration that God
would not take her.
Hospice came with their caring staff and
on July 1st,

Mom's body finally let loose of her,
days before she would have turned
100 years old on July 16th.
Mom's friend Katie, with her weak heart and
round-the-clock oxygen mask, remarkably

made it to her August 9th 100th birthday, but died
weeks later.

Mike died in August of 2006
in a plane crash
in the beautiful Rocky Mountains
when he was 54 years old.
Dad died quietly
of a heart attack
at our home in his single bed in
August of 1969, when he was 57 years old.

When Mom died,
we marveled for years, and still do,
that she outlived Dad and Mike and
Mr. Tyndall and so many others
whose sand raced out of their hourglasses
so much faster than Mom's.

I don't know if it's the quality of the sand
or the hourglass
or the foundation on which it sits.
I only know that I will never forget
the year Mr. Tyndall died before my mom.

I Didn't See Her

I didn't see her,
didn't see the face of the older lady
in the aisle next to me
when we were both shopping yesterday
at the Dollar General store,
but her slow, difficult movements brought
sudden images of my Grandma Dunham,

the flowered duster
from the thrift store that opened
around her swollen knees and
the beaded black house slippers
that she wore
every day,
the swollen legs with the blue veins popping
out,
a ragged road map of her painful life.

There she was,
my Grandma Dunham who died
41 years ago,
sometime during the weekend
before the Meals on Wheels lady
found her stone cold
on a dark November Monday morning.

There was no mistaking the weight–laden,
cane–supported shuffle, and
the way she clicked her dentures
when she talked.
The way that,
even though I could not see her grimaced
eyes,

I could feel the sorrow
in her heart and the desperate longing she
felt
for her only two children,
Wilma and Cliff,
whom she had buried
years before.

I could not see these things
as a restless high school teenager,
mindlessly watching the blaring television
during
Grandma's endless story-telling and
quietly flipping through the pages of
the numerous newspapers and magazines
scattered
on Grandma's worn couch
in her small senior citizen's apartment.

Life had not lived me enough
to have the depth of understanding
that deep loss brings,

but right now,
after this sudden pang of
my own longing,

I wish my Grandma were right here again
on her tattered couch,
telling her endless stories,
me, sitting next to her,
holding the rough, arthritic hand I never held,
listening with rapt attention
to the re-telling of
the stories of her beautiful, imperfect life.

Aren't I a Beauty?

In 2005, Mom reluctantly moved
to an assisted living facility
at the encouragement of
my brother, Tom, and me
when she was 95.

She wasn't near death or anything, in fact,
she was remarkably independent,
still painstakingly balancing her checkbook
without a calculator,
sitting at her old secretary with the drop-
down leaf, gently touching the Bic to her
tongue when the ink started to fade,

still ordering her own medicine
and cooking her own meals, although
in her later years,
she was faithfully clipping –
and using –
the newspaper coupons for Senior Citizen's
night at Arby's on Tuesdays and for
some other hamburger joint on Fridays.
She was a Depression–era child, of course,
and liked her meat and potatoes as well as
any Midwestern man.

It was just that Tom lived hours away
and I lived states away. Her next–door
neighbor, Alice,
with whom she had been friends since the
1950's, and on whom Mom was beginning to
rely more and more, moved away,
moved to Indianapolis to be

closer to her daughter.

The last time Mom broke her hip,
she passed out while she was on the phone
with Alice, and her hip broke, or maybe it was
visa-versa. Either way, it was scary.

Scary in the way that Mom was in
excruciating pain and I was at least
a day's travel away.
Scary in the way that with every passing day,
I knew Mom was coming closer and closer
to the end of her life, to the end of being able
to live
alone safely in the home she had loved
and cared for for more than 50 years.

Scary in the way that
Mom knew it, too, in the way that
even though she kept passing out,
she was quietly fighting
to hold on to every ounce of independence
she could muster, to prove
that she could do it, she could live there
alone, she could be the one who would
never need to move.
Many of Mom's close friends
had already moved to that big Assisted Living
Facility
in the sky but Mom
wasn't ready to join them.

We tried to let her stay alone as long
as she wanted. As long as she could be safe,
even though could no longer
get into or out of her cast iron tub,

even though she was no longer safely able to
go up and down the steep basement steps
to her 30 year-old washer and dryer.
But she kept passing out and the doctors
couldn't fix her and then,
Alice moved.

We all tried so hard
to figure out so many other options but
the best thing we came up with was Mom
moving,
packing up a very few of her beloved
life-long possessions and moving
to an assisted living apartment.

She didn't want to move, but for as long as I
could remember,
Mom always said, "When the time comes, I
will do whatever you kids think is best."
We didn't know for sure what was best,
but we were trying. We loved her.
Mom had already experienced
the care of her elders and vowed
she would not
live with either my brother or me.

Mom agreed to sell her house when she knew
she would not be returning.
I cried almost more tears
when we readied Mom's house for sale
than I did when she died. Drawer after
drawer, shelf after shelf, closet after closet
were all those *things*!
All those pieces of
my mom's life. Grandma's china,
Grandpa's railroad lantern,

The tatting, the cross-stitched
tablecloths, the embroidered tea towels
and knitted hats and scarves, apron after
apron,
bedsheet after bedsheet, some still in their
original packaging,
cookbooks galore and mason jars and empty
medicine bottles and empty Cool Whip tubs
because
"I might need them!"

Two old trunks, one trunk that had been
a wedding gift from their 1938 wedding was
filled with ancient family photos
and Dad's WW II Army uniform
and Mom's tiny royal blue velvet wedding
dress with,
what once was, white lace trim.

Among the photos was a beautiful photo of
Mom,
taken in the 1940's.
She looked young and fresh and happy.
Her hair was rich and thick,
her lipstick red and smooth.
She was wearing a pretty
white "peasant-like" top.
Next time I visited Mom at her apartment,
I showed Mom the photo and asked her about
it

Mom explained that when Dad was overseas
during the service, he bought her this blouse
and sent it to her. She obviously loved it, and
Dad,

had her photo taken in it, and sent it
back to Dad.

Mom's face transformed. She was smiling and
her eyes were bright and clear.
She was a young woman in her 30's,
a beautiful newly-wed, a happy military wife,
a yet-to-be parent.

Mom immediately put the photo in the cloth
bag attached to her walker,
anxious to show her photo
to the next person we saw.
"Beth brought me this old photo. It's me!
Aren't I a beauty?"

It was so unlike my mom I almost laughed
every time she said it.
'Round her little dining table
at lunchtime, she showed her photo,
"Aren't I a beauty?"
To the staff one-by-one, as she saw them
in the hallways.

There was something about Mom getting that
photo back that made having moved
to assisted living more tolerable.
Something about being able to show others
that see, she once was this beautiful,
young woman who did not need a walker,
or hearing aids or glasses,
who was not passing out, who was not taking
a laundry list of medications, who was not
falling or breaking bones,
who did not need anyone to help her do
anything,

that reminded us all that she still was that beautiful, strong, independent woman.

No Matter

No matter how great
your day is
this glorious sunny May 13th,
with its happy yellow daffodils and
fragrant purple irises,

with its
unusually amiable children and
smiling drivers waving
you ahead at the four-way stop,

with its quiet,
easy work-day and
its delicious meal
with a sweet glass of red wine
at day's end
with dear friends
at your favorite Italian restaurant,

you, too, will someday be
that one
laid out
motionless,
lifeless,
in your own warm bed
in the beautiful patio home you bought
after downsizing from the two-story home
you and your late husband built
when you were both
in your 40's and thought you had
decades of life
ahead of you.

Or it might be in a white-sheeted bed
at St. Mary-Corwin Medical Center
where scrub-uniformed nurses and C.N.A.'s
tend to you in shifts,
wiping your brow,
bending the plastic straw toward
your dry mouth,
until your cracked lips lose
their ability to suck and
your beating heart loses its ability to
beat,
and your essence takes leave
of the tired body
it no longer needs.

Or it might be
in the warmly decorated room of
Sangre de Cristo Hospice's inpatient unit
or in any lovely hospice unit
across this nation or maybe
in England,
where hospice care started,
where wives and husbands and children and
nieces and nephews and grandchildren and
sisters and brothers and
friends and lovers and
all who loved you and
some who really didn't,
take vigil
at your quiet bedside,

pacing,
reading,
crying,
singing,
praying,

sleeping,
laughing,
doing

nothing,

until,
like every other living being
in this miraculous universe,
you die.

Whenever or wherever
it happens,
people who know you will marvel
at the fact that

they had just seen you or
just talked with you or
just read your words or
just heard your music or
just left your side
as though

seeing or hearing someone or
reading their words or
hearing their music or
leaving their side
could preclude
their dying.

May you take in
this one breath and
luxuriate in its beauty.

May your heart feel full
with the love of those

who surround you.

May your passage
from this life
to what lies ahead

be one of deep meaning,
beauty,
grace, and
lasting peace.

Mike, Beth's Late Husband

Aunt Mary and Uncle Dan

Beautiful Mom

Beth, her parents, and her Grandma Dunham

Lean Into Compassion

Yarmouk and All the Rest

How can I even think
of buying a new water hose
for the young evergreens
in my arid Colorado backyard
when the people in Yarmouk
and all the rest

of those war-torn countries
go hours or days or weeks
without drinkable water,

leaning weakly against stone walls,
lying quietly amongst
their remaining
somber family members
under tattered rough blankets,
shivering in fear
and hopelessness?

How can I stand for hours
in the light of
my open Maytag refrigerator door,
perusing shelf upon shelf
of fresh vegetables and cold milk,
when the people in Yarmouk
and all the rest

are eating grass from the streets
in a desperate effort to
stay alive,
fainting from hunger,
children leaning into
their weary mothers, whining

after days with no real
sustenance?

How can I luxuriate near the furnace vent,
basking in the waves of
forced air gas heat on a cold January day,
when the people in Yarmouk
and all the rest

are chopping and burning their furniture,
huddling closely in small groups,
rubbing their rough palms together
over the flames
of their lives?

How can I appreciate the luxury
of my American freedom
and the sense of security
behind my Yale
deadbolt-locked front door
when terrorists and
radicals are working every day
to gain strongholds in Yarmouk
and all the rest,

destroying treasured artifacts,
city infrastructures,
valuable resources,
and precious, meaningful lives?

Things Her Unborn Baby Said

I chose you and Daddy to be
my beautiful parents
a very long time ago,

patiently lingering in the sweet stillness
of that place
where souls wait in hushed silence.

I paused,

coming into your lives
with perfect timing.

From the moment
my tiny life began
in the richness of your hearts,
we belonged
to each other.

Nestling into your warmth, I was
growing and expanding,
doubling and quadrupling and
quadrupling again until

my tiny heart was beating and my
eyes and mouth and
fingers and toes appeared
seemingly from nowhere
and I was moving them all and

reaching and stretching and
kicking and bending
all the while listening

to the whooshing of
your steady heartbeat.

It was all happening so fast and
before I knew it,
my thumb found its way
into my mouth and I
tasted its softness,
all the while

floating in the sweet ocean of
your growing belly.

I heard your precious singing and I felt
Daddy's ear close to mine,
pressing gently against my soft head,
his breathing slow and quiet,
savoring his precious gift,
smiling sweetly in anticipation of
our glorious meeting.

Sometimes it felt like time

stood

still

when we were all listening
to one another,

so much in love
with the moment, and with
each other.

Until
that one day

I left,

guided swiftly
into the channel of bright light,
joining the love once again
from where
we all come and to where
we will all return again.

So beautiful,
this light,
this peace,
this all–encompassing love,
it was as though
we had all always known
each other
and the depth
of this beautiful, sacred never–ending
love.

(Written for a friend)

Never Enough Blankets

I am mindlessly driving
up Greenwood Avenue
this cold, cloudy, pre–snowstorm Saturday
afternoon
on the way home from an enjoyable
Christmas party
with hospital volunteers, sleepy,

tummy filled with
tossed salad, warm fried chicken, baked ham,
fresh green beans and sweet
marble cake with thick white icing when

I pass the local soup kitchen.
Men and women in coats,
some heavy, some not,
line the bench in front of the building like
birds on a wire, leaning
against the brick with eyes closed, leaning
against each other, curled
atop piles of old blankets or
sleeping bags.

My warm Buick shows
the outside temperature is 39 degrees.
How does it come to be
that I can drive
this warm, comfortable car
to my warm, comfortable home and
luxuriate in front of my
bright, blinking, flat screen TV
while lying under
my warm, comfortable blanket,

by my warm, comfortable fireplace,
watching romantic old movies, snacking on
cookies or grapes or leftover pot roast or
pecans or
chocolate or cheese cubes or potato chips or
warm,
fresh bread, drinking warm, comforting tea,
while others
cannot?

A month ago I took garbage bags full of
winter scarves, gloves, warm sweaters, coats
and
warm, wool, winter hats to
the local homeless agency
in hopes they could provide
some measure of physical comfort
to those living on the street
in the dead of a cold Colorado winter,

and in hopes that knowing someone cares
about their physical well–being,
might also offer some measure of spiritual
comfort
to those struggling to find their way
in a life that is different
from those who do not have to wonder
where they will sleep or eat
this cold December night.

Thoughts I Cannot Share

Even when the worst
criminal, the murderer,
the guy who took out
his entire family because
he was convinced
they had wronged him
and that only their deaths
could right the pain
he carried so deeply
in his heart,

clinging to that hatred,
the same way the cute towheaded toddler
he once was
clung to the soft blue blanket
his sweet Gramma gave him
when he was one,
toddling through
the rooms of his small home,
dragging his blanket over
thick shag carpet and
the flower–patterned linoleum of
their dark kitchen,

even when that guy
and his equally homicidal buddy,
escaped from prison
in the heat of summer
after years of incarceration
with the craft and ease
of MIT engineers,
and wandered
through thick brush

and deeply forested woods
for days and days,
traumatizing families living
in the area,
taxing hundreds of
law enforcement officers,
wasting millions of dollars
in the massive effort
to find him,

I worried
about him, that guy
who had murdered, taken a life that was not
his
to take,
caused pain for so many and
endless heartache for
those who once loved him.

Did he feel
regret that he left
the prison that was providing
for his every need,
the greasy hamburgers,
the tasteless peas,
the cold cement
underfoot and
the thin mattress
at night where he
slept minimally,
spending long hours imagining a life
outside?

Once outside the prison walls,
did he fear for his life
every single moment, suffering

a sick stomach,
starving or limping in pain
after tripping over
that large downed branch
in the middle of a dark, wet night
knowing full well that
so many people wished
for his capture
and demise?
Was his back
sore and scraped and wrenched
in pain after
days of wide-eyed
discomfort lying on
a bed of dirt piles with
a rock pillow?

Even though I am here,
on this side

of those prison walls, meeting
my Sunday morning coffee group,
playing Handel with my funny
string ensemble, volunteering
with the local Catholic hospital, and
have never been on the other side

of those loud, clanking, heavy steel bars,
or experienced the
unbearable pain of
losing a loved one
at the hand of another,

when I remember family stories
of the toddler me,
thumb in mouth,

whining, dragging my soft pink blanket
across thick shag carpet and
flowered kitchen linoleum, I know that,
like all of us,

there is a part of that guy
in me
and a part of me
in him and,

I admit
that I was just as relieved
when he was captured alive
that he was finally
safe,

as I was that
the people he traumatized
were safe,
too.

On Losing Your Loves

When your beautiful mother crossed
to the other side,
the heavens opened wide,
billowy white clouds gently parting,
revealing a brilliant blue sky and
blazing warm golden sun.

Bands of angels,
with your sister and father
clinging tightly to one another,
gently floated together
from the beauty of the place
where love and life
never end.

Arm-in-arm,
wing-in-wing,
soft palms gently reaching
for their love,
they tenderly clasped
your mother's small, tired hand and
together, lifted

with the beauty and grace
of a quiet white dove,
to the heavens from whence they came,
and to where,
one-by-one,
we will all
meet again,
with the sweetest,
happiest,
surest

embrace.

(Written for a friend.)

Two Kids Bombed the Boston
Marathon This Week

Two kids bombed
the Boston Marathon this week.

Three people died,
scores were injured,
two brothers each lost
part of a leg and
all I can think about is

the two kids.

Nineteen and twenty–six
years old they were.

Nineteen,
the age I was as a sophomore
at Indiana University,
playing records all night
in my dorm room, listening to
Chicago, Boz Skaggs, Stevie Wonder,
partying with the guys
down the hall.

When I was twenty–six,
the girls at the office
introduced me to Mike,
gathering in small groups
after our first date,
whispering and giggling.

Two kids bombed
the Boston Marathon this week.

The older one died
in a violent shootout
with police who
gathered by the hundreds,

dressed in tactical gear,
crouching behind cars, sometimes
running down the street
en masse,
weapons drawn.

I imagine the older bomber
as a baby,
his parents swaddling him tightly
in the softest blue blanket,
laying him gently
in the crib at the foot of their bed,
as they lay sleepless,
listening to the sweet coos
of their first child,
praying for his long, happy life.

Two kids bombed
the Boston Marathon this week.

The nineteen year-old,
the little brother,
the bomber who didn't get killed,
lies quietly in a Boston hospital bed,
freshly pressed white sheets
wrapped tautly around the firm mattress
under his injured young body,
security guards blocking
the exit from his room.

In the darkness of night,
the young bomber
squeezes his eyes tightly,
holding back tears,
remembering
his older brother,
wishing they were together again,
wrestling, throwing fake punches,
dreaming of beautiful women.

In the darkness of night,
in the other hospital wing,

bombing victims turn restlessly
in their hospital beds, sleepless,
pulling at their IV tubing,
mindlessly turning
magazine pages,
pushing the call light for
more cold water or
pain medicine.

Two kids bombed
the Boston Marathon this week.

Their parents, separated
by hardship and pain,
cling tightly to their remaining children,
two daughters,
and to the reality that
no soothing maternal touch
or paternal show of strength
can ever heal
their broken lives.

(Author's Note: I was ambivalent about printing this poem, fully aware that many innocent people have suffered lifelong physical and emotional pain as a direct result of the terrorist acts committed by these two young men. I mean no disrespect to anyone personally affected by these violent acts and certainly do not condone violence in any form.

I offer my deepest sympathy to the families of those who have lost loved ones or lost limbs or peace of mind as a result of the Boston Marathon bombing. My hope is that all those personally affected continue to receive the emotional, physical and spiritual support they need.

When I first learned the ages of the two bombers, I was struck by their relative youth. It was difficult for me not to remember what my life was like at their respective ages and wonder how different my life would be with a completely different life experience.)

It Seems Possible

It seems possible that
the cricket I hear singing
tonight
along the Arkansas River
this gorgeous August evening

is the same one I heard singing
by Agnes Hough's lake
in 1965,
while my mom
and her Beta Sigma Phi sisters
met over coffee and Jello mold
in Agnes' sun room,

and I sat quietly
by the lake,
mesmerized by the huge bullfrogs
and silent fish
nipping at the water's green surface
making concentric circles

until Mom,
or one of her sisters, came calling,
fearing my demise.

It seems just as possible that
this persistent cricket
and its family
are the same ones who lived

in the window well
beneath my Indiana childhood
second-story bedroom

on Cartwright Drive,

singing me to sleep on
hot, muggy, summer nights
while the drone of the metal exhaust fan
at the opposite end of the dormer bedroom
roared hot air across
my damp sheets and whirred
the cricket song deep
into the dark night.

It also seems possible
that this cricket,
the same one from the Arkansas River,
the same one from Agnes Hough's lake,
the same one from my childhood bedroom
window well,

is the same one who started singing
when my dear friend, Dorothy, died
tonight,
in an Indiana hospital,

surrounded by her loving family
gently calling her name,
tenderly caressing her
forehead,
holding the hand that had,
so many times,
held theirs,

wishing them comfort and
strength and
grace, while

outside the hospital window,

a chorus of crickets filled the summer air
in celebration of a life
well–lived,

like the wonder of a woman by a beautiful
Colorado river and
the joy of a child by a lake or
the peace of a youngster at rest
at the end of a happy summer day.

(Written for a friend.)

God Bless the Cleaners

who come in
after the mass shooting
at the social service agency, the high school
or Planned Parenthood or
the Army base or the concert in Paris,

after the suicide of someone's
quiet father or sweet aunt or lonely
grandchild,
after the murder-suicide of
your sunny neighbors, stalwarts of the church
and
proud civic leaders.

On rainy Monday mornings the cleaners
come, working,
on hands and knees, sometimes
crossing themselves, kissing the gold crucifix
from their godparents, tucking it tightly
beneath their cotton shirts,

wiping hard, wrenching tears with their long-
sleeved gray
uniform work shirts, masking their noses and
mouths to
hide the stench of death and Clorox Bleach
before
scrubbing,

first gently,
then with gritted-teeth vigor, then with
closed-eye resolve,

they clean

blood-spattered walls and windows,
dry erase boards and laptop computers,
pink-smeared linoleum or
beautiful red oak hardwood floors,
institutional hard plastic chairs or patterned
couches,
round café tables and wooden doorframes,

dipping their gloved hands repeatedly
into the once-clear, warm water,
squeezing their sponges and rags
tighter and tighter until
the water finally disappears
over the buckets,
onto the floors,
into the rooms and
the stains have vanished and
there is nothing left to clean
but their minds and
their clothes for the next day.

Just Being

It was a lovely Colorado September morning,
a crisp dawn with achingly blue skies,
a transitional kind of day where gentle winds
were blowing
in the next season, ushering out summer,
ushering in
what followed, when I read
the e-mail that another sweet friend, a peer,
a tennis buddy of Mike's,
had died. This time, cancer. Many times,
cancer.

His wife, late wife I guess, now, sent the e-
mail
a month later, on what would have been,
Brad's 61st birthday. An impossibly
young end to a meaningful life and a lovely
36-year marriage.

Sighing deeply, I rose slowly
from my office chair, pacing the floors,
looking out the windows
at the continuous white jet streams overhead,
the golden leaves swirling in the street,
a whirlpool of nameless energy,
the neighbor's happy dogs, barking, and
running and
chasing each other endlessly.

Where do these lives go
when they stop being present here?
What happens to the beautiful energy of my
friends

and the incredible love of my husband and
the beautiful grace of my parents and aunts
and uncles and
grandparents and in-laws and dogs and cats?

One warm spring Friday,
I paid a surprise visit to my 95 year-old mom
at her assisted living facility, where she was
sitting in a semicircle with other residents,
reaching her arms overhead,
kicking out her legs, happily working her
still-functioning body.

She glowed when she saw me and cheerfully
left the group, calling my name in surprise,
walking out to greet me with arms wide.

We walked arm-in-arm to her room,
spending the day talking,
going out for lunch, just
being.

It was the best day
for both of us and Mom talked about it
for months. Remember that day
when you surprised me during exercise class
and we went out to Bob Evans for potato
soup?

I like to think that this is what it is.
That even when someone dies,
every now and then,
they surprise you
on a warm Friday afternoon
whether you can see them or not,
and spend the day with you,

talking,
eating potato soup,
just
being.

(Written for a friend.)

Blessings Be

To the short–sleeved man sitting
alone on the concrete bench
at the bus stop
this cold December day,
Blessings be,
and to

the single parent of the tired toddler who,
at the end
of a very long shopping day, tearfully
really, really, really
wants that too–expensive toy,
Blessings be,
and to

the elderly gentleman
who approached the hospital
information desk but needed to sit
for hours in the lobby
trying to remember
his dear friend's last name,
Blessings be,
and to

the stray black dog
darting across this busy street,
rattling through alleyways,
picking through garbage,
settling himself onto piles of
old newspapers,
Blessings be,
and to

the newly bereaved
experiencing their first holiday without
their beloved friend or family member.
Blessings be,
and to

the pained souls
huddled together
on the other side
of the globe,
and on this side,
without food or shelter or
spiritual nourishment,
Blessings be,
and to

those with all material possessions
and love beyond measure,
but without a degree of hope
or gratitude,
Blessings be.

Lean Into Hope

This Spring

Earlier this spring they came
wandering out from their closed homes,
shading their eyes from the bright sun
ambling sluggishly
like huge brown bears
after a long hibernation.

Different shapes and sizes
making their way
to the Y, or to the noisy workout center
with the mirror–lined walls.

They drove across town or
across the street like Muslims
honoring the call to prayer,
not five times a day,
sometimes not even once
a month, but still
they came,
baring their white legs
in fresh jogging shorts,
toting water bottles,
short white towels thrown
over their shoulders
masking as athletes
training for a marathon.

Outside the gym,
daffodils stretched
their long necks towards

an impossibly blue sky,
after working their way through

hard brown soil,
bursting from the white bulbs
planted last fall,
six inches deep.

Bright yellow blooms swayed
in the March breeze,
urging the athletes on,
smiling like proud parents
on game day,
high–fiving each other
as the treadmills lurched forward.

This spring,
this shiny rebirth of green
and blue and yellow
launches us all
forward,
pushes us towards
that imagined life
of our dreams that
laid sleeping under thick quilts
in the darkness of winter.

The Host

In this body, there is no room
for cancer. There is no room
for dark little cells, shivering in
tight little groups, hiding in
warm places, tucked under
rolls of fat or lumped together
against strong organs without
invitation. Go find
your own little support group for cells
outcast from their host and
share your sad stories, drinking
beer and eating stale pretzels in
some darkened room in the old bar
at the end of the dirt road
with yellowed wallpaper,
torn sheer curtains and broken lights that
flicker and sway from the ceiling
when visitors slam
the heavy wooden door.

In this body, there is no room
for cancer. There is no room
for extra guests in the spare
bedroom or room for one last can
of Campbell's soup
for the pantry. There is no room
for one more pair of warm
navy blue knee socks
in the dresser drawer or one more
winter coat in the hall closet.

In this body, there is no room
for cancer, so skedaddle on outta here,
"Take the Last Train to Clarksville,"

"Make Like a Tree and Leaf," and
get the hell out of here!

In this body there is
no
room
for
cancer!

*("The Host" was written after the author's
diagnosis of and treatment for an early-stage
cancer in 2012. She is grateful to have
remained cancer-free but extends healing
thoughts and support to others in the midst of
cancer treatment.)*

What If We Jumped?

I don't want to write
about what could be
lurking in the dark
shadows behind
that big chair or
on the other side
of my quiet bedroom door.

It might be the high ledge
of my nightmares
from which height I never fall but
from whose dreams I awaken
in a heart–pounding sweat.

What if you took my hand and
we jumped together
from my imaginary ledge and
smiled at the beauty
of the colored rock canyon
as we floated
like parachuted skydivers
gently down,
carefully alighting on
the softest, sweetest bed
of fragrant wildflowers?

In Gratitude for the Sunny Side

Oh My God!
On the other side of
the overwhelming,
all–consuming darkness of
anxiety or depression or
grief or pain or loneliness or
fear or illness
or self–doubt is
the Holy Grail!

Is gleaming Emerald City,
the tall sparking, engraved trophy,
the framable gold–embossed
Certificate of Acceptance,
the dozen long–stemmed roses
wrapped in a bow
placed gently in your proud arms,
the luscious aromatic 20–pound turkey
sliding out of the oven
at noon on Thanksgiving Day while
your family smiles their loving approval.

On the other side
is the 20–pound weight–loss
after a determined effort at
improved health and
an easy breath
at the flower–lined spa
after a glorious hot stone massage
and the sweetest celebratory glass of
sparkling champagne
and rich dark chocolates
with your beloved

on a sunny veranda
in the south of France, or

maybe just on
your sweet backyard flagstone patio,
where happy yellow wildflowers sway
in the early morning breeze,
in communion with you and your
new-found location
on the sunny side.

What If This Is Not the Last?

My beloved white-haired friends lean
in close around
the crowded corner table
at The Daily Grind Coffee Shop
sacred Sunday mornings,

sipping black coffee and Jasmine tea,
sharing poppyseed bread,
back yard tomatoes and sacred stories.

The reverence of
our deep sharing moves quietly
in waves around the table,
a tangible swell of emotion when

one laments
about life in the sixth decade, or maybe
the seventh or eighth.

This is our last house,
the last
car we will ever buy,
the last time we will be able
to walk the length of that
beautiful trail or tolerate the duration of
that three-hour movie or
the day-long museum tour.

This is the last
side-by-side Maytag refrigerator or
upright Hoover vacuum cleaner we will need
with the few remaining colorful beads left
on our designated abacuses.

I stand up boldly and say,
what if it is?

What if the last house we bought
is the last house we buy?
No more fussing with
banks or realtors or
title companies with names like
law partners.

What if our last meanderings
through the appliance store
were the last times we had to study and
bicker and debate about

the right one or
the best one or
the one that would last
the longest or best meet
our needs,
opening and closing the doors
of each appliance to assess
the storage or decide if
the light really went off when
the door closed? But

what if tomorrow,
we are still walking
that long, beautiful prairie trail,
still laughing out loud
in the crowded movie theater,
still haggling with the young
tie-clad car dealer about
our next luxurious car?

What if, next year, on a whim,
we sell the house we just bought,
move to the Caribbean,
leave our dear friends and family, and
live out our days
in the warmth of the sun
and the white of the ocean sand?

Or what if we just move
down the street
to that sweet apartment complex,
the one with
fresh flowers in the lobby
and the piano-playing couple,
laughing, and dancing around
each other, sharing a happy musical duet?

Or what if, next summer,
we trade in our new car
for a newer one,
the one we said
we would never buy but
always wanted?

What if,
as life slowly evolves,
passing quietly from winter to spring and
spring to summer,
it is gentler than we could have imagined and

we are happier with our
lasts or our still-haves,
than we ever thought possible,
leaning way back
in our plush leather La-Z-Boys,
shaking our heads in wonder

at the ones who are still lamenting
about their lasts?

My Beautiful Life

On this January First,
on this first day of this
New Year, 2015,
I can erase,
if I want,

memories of seemingly
poor choices,

painful words with a beloved
family member,
ego–filled thoughts about
my self– importance and self–
righteousness,

or I can erase,
if I want,
memories of potentially wonderful choices
I feared and avoided,

a new relationship,
travel to distant lands,
moving past,
skipping ahead in line like
an inpatient shopper,
assuming the best choice was
surely not the one
I held
in my hand.

Or I can erase,
if I want,
memories of world tragedies,

war, famine, Ebola,
beheadings, tornadoes, floods, mud
slides, fires, hate
of policemen and women and
others who do not look
like me, or hate of ones who
do not love the ones
I love, fatal
plane crashes –
families and friends of 162
AirAsia passengers and crew wait
in prayer as
pieces of metal and
floating bodies are plucked from
the turbulent Java Sea.

Or I can keep,
if I want,
sweet memories of
visits with long–time friends,
horseback riding,
walks along beautiful Lake Michigan and
along the beautiful Arkansas River,

loving family celebrations of
graduations, precious holiday dinners
at my big brother's log cabin,
lovely string music with dear friends,
tea with others on warm spring days
and weekend Scrabble
competitions in the dark
of winter
with my sweet neighbors.

But,

my heart wants to
hold them all,
the memories of
the love and hate,
the war and peace,
the life and death,

keeping them filed loosely
in metal card boxes,
withdrawing them gingerly in time
with thumb and forefinger,

gluing them neatly,
or sometimes sloppily,
onto large poster boards
like a school project or
weaving them quietly
into soft fabric,
designing the fettered pattern
that is
my beautiful life.

In Her Dreams

In her dreams,
she is traveling
to Europe, touring
beautiful museums and ancient castles,
walking along luscious green isles or running
her hand slowly across the massive marble
columns
of breath–taking Roman Cathedrals.

In her dreams,
back home, after years without her beloved
Nikki,
she is adopting a new dog
from the shelter, one who
will not release her gaze, one who presses
its soft fur gently
against the metal enclosure, slowly
wagging its tail, hoping fate will
entice even the most uncertain visitor.

In her dreams,
she drops
all responsibilities and vows
to take the next six months,
or however long it takes, to drive across
the country, stopping
to visit every special friend or family member
along the way.

In her dreams,
when the next person dies,
whether the death is sudden or
long–expected,

whether the person is someone she loves
or someone she has never met,
she makes a pact
that she will awaken
from her dream, that she will not
wait another second to live
the life that is waiting for her,
that is playing out in her mind every time
she closes her eyes, the life that her brother
told her to live after he put her
on the plane to fly back to Colorado after
their mom died. She can still hear
his words echoing in her mind, see them
drifting across
the busy road,
through the airport terminal, down the
narrow
aisle of the tubular plane:
"Now go live your life."
And so,
she does, or maybe
she is still
dreaming.

*(Thank you to Greg Gibson for his literary
input on "In Her Dreams.")*

The Day She Wrote a Poem in Which No One Died

It was a March Tuesday morning and
she was standing in her kitchen,
bright sunlight daring her to have
a negative thought, challenging her to ignore
the multiple beautiful tiny rainbows
floating on her textured walls cast from the
large brilliant crystal hanging
in her living room window.

KCFP was playing her favorite Handel Sonata,
the laundry was folded, hung and put away
and there was nothing left
but to enjoy this lovely day
as she wished, maybe with a walk
along the Arkansas River or perhaps
a quick trip to the enchanting
Garden of the Gods or a rare visit
with a sweet out-of-town friend.

Whichever she decided, or didn't, not one
dead person or funeral or thought of
bereavement or grief or chronic illness was
allowed
into her heart or into her sunny home or
happy yard on this day, where her Ash tree
and steady green
pines were already
budding, were pushing out the tiniest forms
of new life, bursting from what once seemed
dead.

This Day Was Different

Even though the morning sunlight filtered
through her blinds
the same way as always,
patterning itself on her yellow bedroom walls,
across the snowy mountain art print,
softly over her polar bear quilt
like every Tuesday morning,
this day was different.

Different in the way
her feet easily found the carpeted floor,
in the way her body
eased itself from supine to upright and
in the way her shoulders threw themselves
back
even before
she was fully awake,
before she had mapped out her plan
for the day.

Brushing her teeth,
she looked in the mirror
at her smiling face and noticed
that even her waves of brown hair
had fallen gently into place
before a brush had even touched them and
before she had considered
what clothing would best suit the day's
weather.

Eating her granola and blueberries,
watching the morning news,
she noticed that even the national stories
were

more hopeful,
fewer people were killed and even the
weather forecaster
forecasted nothing but sunny skies
from one nation to the next,
smiling that her hand–held electronic clicker
was
rotating the weather maps
as it should.

Heading down the street in her clean Buick,
through the green lights,
past the smiling crossing guard and the
skipping uniformed school children,
she knew, but need not know why,
this day was different.

About the Author:

Beth Bricker Davis has been a lifelong writer and has found great solace using the written word as an emotional outlet. She has worked in the social work field for more than thirty years, the last eight and a half years as a hospice counselor. Davis is retired and lives in Pueblo, Colorado, to where she moved in 2000, from her home state of Indiana. When she is not writing, she enjoys playing violin in a 12–member classical string ensemble, Sunday Strings, which she co–founded in 2000, and doing volunteer work for a local hospice and hospital.

Davis published her first book of poetry, *Aspen Leaves in October, Poems of Life, Love, and Loss,* in 2013, which was a book of grief poems written after the sudden death of her husband, Dr. Mike Davis, in 2006.

Made in the USA
Middletown, DE
04 May 2021